What Life Is Like Here on Earth

What Life Is Like Here on Earth

poems

Katherine Riegel

Sheila-Na-Gig Editions

ISBN: 978-1-962405-73-7
Library of Congress Control Number: 9781962405737

Sheila-Na-Gig Editions
Russell, KY
Hayley Mitchell Haugen, Editor
www.sheilanagigblog.com

Acknowledgments

Bear Paw Arts Journal: "Everybody Walks in England,"
   "Parfumerie Magique"
Does It Have Pockets?: "My Entrance to the Otherworld is in
   Illinois," "She Couldn't Understand My Words but I Still
   Wish I Could Unsay Them," "What Life Is Like Here on
   Earth"
Elysium Review: "The Afterlife of Dogs"
Hole in the Head Review: "In Which I Consider Depression and
   the Fall of Humanity in the Context of My Dog's
   Misbehavior," "Requirements," "We're All Standing in
   Line for That"
Inkfish Magazine: "Noctalgia," "This World Always Offers
   Reasons for Despair," "What the Insomniac Thinks"
JAKE: "Reading My Living Room Floor Like Tea Leaves"
On the Seawall: "Good Girls, Good Mothers," "Talking to
   Animals"
One Art: "When I Stopped"
Passengers Journal: "1001 Nights"
Quartet: "To Myself at Twelve"
Rattle: "Quitter"
SWWIM: "Not Every Body Is This Hard to Carry," "Save What
   You Can"
Thimble: "The Metaphorical Dog," "Time Is Not Real, But
   Scientists Say It Makes No Difference to Us"
Tinderbox Poetry Journal: "Talking"

Abundant gratitude to my writing group—Carolyn Alessio, Maureen Curtin, Deborah Weaver, and Kelly Wilson—whose insight helped inspire and shape these poems.

*for Andy, who insists I don't know how to be cranky
despite all evidence to the contrary*

Contents

What Life Is Like Here on Earth

Some days you wake up and something tiny happens—
you stub your toe on the way to the bathroom
or watch a starving pit bull in one of those awful social media
videos that usually has a happy ending but still syphons
a few minutes of your dear attention and leaves you

with that skinny-sad-dog image branded onto your brain—
and the rest of the day is ruin. You remember how lonely
you are and blame it on your blue-eyed sister dead
from cancer at fifty-eight and maybe it is that,
or maybe it's the juvenile hawk crying and crying

as he flies over the neighborhood, maybe it's your body
throwing another flamboyant fit of ache and fatigue
so you won't be able to plant the wild strawberries
again. Those days your sloppy tears keep coming
back and the phlegm clogs your throat and you blow

your nose 'til it's raw, tell yourself to buck up, the sun is out
and you don't want to get a sinus headache, do you?
Those days you scrabble around for an antidote
to your exile, you research co-housing, fantasize
about gathering a posse of good people to buy

an English manor house and live there together,
filling that old library with eclectic books, walking out
on the lawn like you're wearing empire waist dresses
instead of the roomy jeans and sweatshirts
you always choose. Those days you wait like a dog at the door

for the thing to happen that makes you
forget or reject your loneliness, the thing that doesn't offer
your joints a salve or show your sister in heaven
but happens anyway, without fanfare,
so when you go to bed that night you look at yourself

in the mirror and have to remember why
your eyelids are swollen and your head wool-stuffed,
and you know you made it through another one of those days
still carrying the tin cup you hold out to the world
hoping for something sweet.

Talking to Animals

If you open my head like a flip top
everything will be a green
horizon, corn and soybeans going

on forever, sky generous enough
to hold every loss as lightly
as a frog caged in gentle fingers

and carried back outside to live.
Barn with a white aluminum roof
that amplifies the rain until

the sound is drenching. Horses
lowering their heads to whuffle
for a carrot held on a flat palm,

eyes of every animal I loved and wanted
to be: dog cat raccoon cardinal swan
cheetah, my favorite

because I craved speed. I suppose
people must be there too but I don't
think I ever knew them purely, even

my sister who understood so much
about our childhood and died
before me. I want to believe we will meet

on that old farm in the flatlands,
young again and able, this time,
to hear what the animals say back.

Not Every Body Is This Hard to Carry

Having a body is like dragging around
a huge purse, one of those satchel-sized leather
behemoths that holds everything you could possibly

need: wallet, change purse, sunglasses, pen, lip balm,
clear stream to sit beside, existential crisis, your dead
relatives' voices, doggie poop bags. It's all

in there but you have to root around
for your keys, and while you're pawing through
you find other things you forgot you were carrying:

envelope with a friend's address on it, white-flecked rock
you picked up because it was shaped like a heart.
The thing is fucking heavy, and for some of us

it just gets heavier, and then we discover
we can't run with it, the corners
are soggy with pain, old to-do lists spill

from the top. The body begins to tear,
duct tape doesn't help, it's a struggle to keep
everything where it's supposed to be. Suddenly

your crackling knees insist *I am you* and your mind
says *Fuck off* but then you remember you're actually inside
the ginormous purse and oh-my-god there's

the bike you rode at fourteen, hot wind in your face,
the turquoise ring you can no longer wear on your swollen fingers,
and at the very bottom a weedy path

you know you have to walk—you want
to walk—if you can just get it together, chivvy yourself
out of your chair, not always hopeful but alive, still alive.

1001 Nights

I tell myself stories in my sleep. Sometimes
I wake wishing for a donkey to put my arms around,
its head resting on my shoulder, its love
so loud the whole world knows.

In the afternoon I wish for hummingbirds'
aerial acrobatics above my head, sacred,
and me in my rocking chair on the patio
somehow significant. All day the bells ring

and someone wishes. Scheherazade tells her stories
to stay alive every night. The powerful always
want to kill someone. In my stories
everyone lives and treasure is everywhere:

afternoon light like a crescendo, mountains
bowing to one another across the valleys,
a new color discovered every day.

On screens small and large the beatings go on
but at night the stories come in like the tides.

Good Girls, Good Mothers

Mothers who had to wear white gloves but wouldn't
force their daughters to. Mothers who played
field hockey and basketball. Mothers who didn't know
whether a body was made to hurl

into the world or to be viewed through glass
and dusted daily. Mothers who married
before sex, who were taught nothing,
who knew little of the desire they saw floating

through the air like bubbles. Mothers who
smiled at innuendos but never understood them, even
after their children had begun to learn the languages
of other people's bodies. Mothers who starved

themselves to fit into narrow-waisted white
wedding dresses they kept forever because they were
supposed to. Mothers who divorced, mothers who
didn't. Mothers who tried to do the right thing.

Mothers who held their children when they shivered
and broke hairbrushes on their backsides,
laughing out loud as the punishment turned
ridiculous, pieces of plastic and bristles flying

across the bed. Mothers who never joked
about animals, mothers who taught how to cook
and sew, mothers who became nurses instead
of doctors. Mothers who loved snow-capped mountains

and sang songs from *The Sound of Music*.
Mothers who read books, mothers who relished
plunging their hands into the dark earth to bring forth
tomatoes and green peppers. Mothers who named the birds

then dressed for cocktail parties like a knight
for battles. Ghost mothers standing in fields
on the other side of cancer, waiting to receive us, especially
the ones whose mothers couldn't love them enough,

the living who fear what happens after, the suffering
and the shamed and those who made mistakes—
which is all who were born into this world,
all who will fall or crash or sigh into the next.

Reading My Living Room Floor Like Tea Leaves

The dog got anxious again and shredded a catalog
we left on the coffee table for just this purpose,
strewing irregular bits of colored paper

across the floor. Plus-sized sweaters
in awful turquoise and fuchsia
leer from muted beige swiped with rust and sage,

a rug purchased specifically to hide dirt and dog hair
and the occasional spilled milky tea. Clothes in my size
are almost always ugly, as though loving

chocolate means you can't want to look decent,
and though I generally don't care because
I'm sporting dubious spots of canine drool

and don't have anywhere to go anyway, I will never
wear fuchsia even if the damned world *is* ending. Soon
I'll have to get down on my hands and knees to pick up

the multitudinous pieces, as the fancy German vacuum
I bought in a rare moment of financial windfall
has a delicate throat not suited to paper,

and because my back and various other body parts
squeal when I do this, for a moment I contemplate
ordering one of those long-handled sticks with a lever

for grabbing what's beyond reach and getting it delivered
because, let's face it, I'm not lazy but I am continually tired,
my energy worn down to the cords

by an immune-chewing illness I contracted at the fresh age
of twenty-one. Most days I'm faking it worse than
the models in that catalog who pretend to be delighted

by their homely clothes and bullet-proof bras,
probably stuck listening to the photographer say
they're lucky to be big girl models

because they don't have to diet, when they're thinking
they still have to keep themselves just the right side
of size 16 and never lose that hourglass shape.

Today I hauled myself up off the couch
and crossed the room and for a moment
I discerned a shape in the bits of paper:

a scale, the old kind with the hanging platforms
to weigh coins, and I thought about what we do to balance
should with *need*, who the screens tell us to be

with who we are, and if we have to rip something up
to get through the day and eat some of it too then so be it,
chance cages us too often and living is messy.

In Cyclic Time the World Never Ends

Long before it was easy to peer at Stonehenge
from the portal of my laptop on a sacred solstice

I dreamt huge slabs standing mysterious
in the cornfields near my house. Why not

an Illinois farm girl, why not me with my head
full of moors and stout stone castles? I wanted

places where the worlds thinned,
escaping to the oldest tree on our property

for my rituals with lucky rock and four-leaf clover.
The stories start with a child wandering

somewhere she doesn't understand: thistle-pocked fields
concealing white birds or fairies, glittering dancers

glimpsed through a dark doorway, the still pool
reflecting something different every time.

I want to believe every augury means
we'll get a future full of fish and grain

rather than salted streets and killing
smoke like our current seers foretell.

But the clock inside me ticks backwards
and I wouldn't mind finding out when I die

that every door leads to the past,
even the door that led me here, to this life,

and its landscape littered with precious things
I am helpless to save because they have already been

saved, or lost, though they haunt someone else's
serpentine dreams under stars not yet mapped.

In Which I Consider Depression and the Fall of Humanity in the Context of My Dog's Misbehavior

The chemical make-up of my brain is part lemon, part lost
child, part maple seed spinning to earth. Did hunter-gatherers
suffer depression? I read somewhere our Neanderthal genes

predispose us to it, but I also read trauma is handed down
like family china you never use but cannot bring yourself
to give away. Who doesn't have trauma in their family tree?
Violence regular as seasons, hurt we learned early
never to talk about. I want to believe agriculture ruined

paradise—the labor that stooped our backs, the overseers
feeling power take root in their stomachs with its parasitic
poison, and money money money my god money—but maybe

we killed off the mammoths and giant sloths millennia earlier
like some toxic human spill. When I put down

the goodness in myself and can't find it again,
I travel back through time
searching for the source of evil. What does it feel like

to know you deserve to be alive? Even when the slow boat
of my brain is making good headway, the spray cool
and sparkling, all I can do is fail

to think about it. And yet my love
flailing down the path as our dog dragged him
and his half-invented word that made me laugh
so hard I could not move my feet:

I almost went flugeling he said
and even remembering
my stomach contracts, my mouth
stretches in that weird miracle of biology and culture
that must prove some kind of divinity
still lives in us, no matter how far we keep falling.

My Entrance to the Otherworld Is in Illinois

Hawthorns ruled the slope we called *The Wild Area,*
a green mess from the west side of the house down
to the horse pasture. I loved this space
because my father couldn't tame it,
and when I scrambled under the blackberry canes
and crawled on hands and knees into that breathing shadow

I was untamed too. I never feared those fairy tale thorns,
but I never touched the sharp points
with my fingertip, either. I was so young I thought
hawthorns only grew on our farm, bloomed only
so my mother could lean out the upstairs window
and say, *My! Smell that, will you?*

      We drove away
in the spring, my father too afraid
of the life the rest of us loved. Four kids,
ten to eighteen, and a wife who hoped
this sacrifice might finally blunt his anger.

My secret heart remains there, impaled,
caught between that old world of true stories
and this one I have come to fear
made of metal and glass and humming wires
to swallow wind and leaves alike.

Do those hawthorns still open their fists of wild
blossoms each spring, casting the scent that could take me
through the gate and home? *Once upon a time
we drove away,* I begin. But that is all I know.

Requirements

My dog is at the vet to be spayed.
A document entitled "symptoms" is open
on my screen, though it also lists
medications and side effects and possible

diagnoses. Two friends live with MS
and two with autoimmune diseases carrying
complicated names. My brother
must have his throat stretched from the inside

every year. All my siblings remember
ailments our parents and grandparents had
better than I do, though now
my sister with her family knowledge

is gone: cancer, echoing down the generations
from our grandmother to her daughter to hers,
all three women with the same first
names. How delicate these bodies are,

thrown this way and that with every tide.
Imperfection built in, so easy to harm,
like the poor dogwood sapling I planted
in too much sun, its leaves burned and curling

around the edges. I want to line up
my loved ones and touch each of them
with a wand: *you will be well, and you,*
and you, and you. An epidemic of wellness.

See? I would be a benevolent god. My love
would not require suffering. But didn't I drop off
my sweet dog at the vet, knowing
what would happen to her there?

The Loss Game

I saw the ophthalmologist after the sun
scraped my eyes, the reflection off old snow
painful even through dark glasses,

eyelids swelling under my fingers
until I had to pull the car over.
That was three months

after my mother died.
When I asked the doctor—
a boy, really, young as snowdrops—

if my grief-wrung tears were the reason
for this new pain,
he looked down, adjusted

his glasses. *It's actually
a dry eye condition*, he said.
Have you ever played

the loss game? If you had to lose
a limb, which one would it be?
If you had to lose a sense?

For me, sight will always
be last. How can I know
the world without vision?

And yet I may grow old,
unlike my mother,
who died, with her senses intact,

of cancer. The boy doctor
did not say he was sorry. *Unfortunately,*
he said, *those are the wrong kind of tears.*

I looked at him across the chasm
of my grief. I looked at him
as he described what I would have

to do, the hot compresses
and eyedrops and all. I knew
I would do anything. I needed

my sight to navigate this new life
as a half-orphan, this life like a room
too dim and full of dangerous edges.

I Was Promised Personal Flying Machines

To see the earth like one of those
drone videos, landscape unrolling below
like the yellowed paper with its pattern of cut holes
moving through my grandfather's antique music box,
notes of air accompanying me, my own flock. I want

even rain to reach me while still in the sky,
for my feet with their roadmaps of pain
never to touch the ground. Didn't I try the high jump

pre-puberty, setting up two-by-fours on hay bales
in the dusty horse arena, running as fast as a freckled
girl could until I planted my foot and reached
with my whole self for those extra inches,
almost feeling a bubble of magic expanding

under my ribcage? Before she died, I told
my mother that what I had wanted most
as a child was a zipline set up in the arena.
She said, "You should have told me! We could
have done that." Had she forgotten

my father's anger that sprang from worry, his
conviction that we were one step from
the lion's red mouth every day, how I froze
when he yelled and learned to make myself
invisible against the dark wood paneling?

Better, better to forget. To believe flight is another
impossibility I might master. To keep believing
the future will bring that freedom, even if
I have to wait for some end to take me tumbling
upward through light and water vapor to new light
so strange no one here has ever even imagined it.

She Couldn't Understand My Words but I Still Wish I Could Unsay Them

When she was young, my dog found a severed
wing at the off-leash park and ran away with it,
finally splashing into a shallow pond, knowing
I wouldn't follow. I don't know why I was so angry.
As if that oar of the air belonged to some kind

of angel, gristle and all. When our mother
told us four kids to jump we knew the right response
was *How high*? Yet she gave us so much freedom
to roam the fields of our rural neighborhood
and decline to attend Sunday School

that when we didn't behave
her wrath was sharp and cold as quartz
and her disappointment one of those tricks
where someone sets you up to fall
backwards over an obstacle. On your ass,

face hot, you had so much to manage
you didn't think to rage back—except our oldest
brother, the one who became a lawyer. Once
he and Mom tried to storm out the same door
and got wedged there for a second, just long enough

they both had to laugh. I did not believe
I wanted a dog to command, a pseudo-child
trained, like I had been, to obey. Maybe I wanted
fairy tale pets so graceful and kind they always
made life easier. But no, I've cleaned up

enough shit and vomit to know real animals
aren't two-dimensional bluebirds singing on your
shoulder, no matter how much Mom loved

that old Disney song—*zippity doo dah!*—she sang
while paddling a canoe or picking raspberries,

happy. When my dog dawdled in that muddy water
I said, *Fine. I don't love you anymore* and turned
my back. Of course that was the trick: walk away
and love will follow, wild and wayward as an angel
who has lost a wing but still hovers just out of sight.

When I Stopped

I never had to beg
for a pony. The horses just

were—muscled motion,
familiar as milkweed

seeds. My mother
had epilepsy and my father

thought that should make
us all as angry as he was,

poor delicate out of control
tyrant with his fists

clenched tight. We lived
so easily then but no one

knew it, the 1970s full
of fear as any decade.

I knew raspberry thorns
and barn smell, freedom

on bike and horseback
and sneakered foot,

place as solid as the ice
in a water bucket come

winter. And then they sold
the horses—I had not known

you could sell family—
and we moved to town.

I always thought that
was when I stopped

trusting I would be
loved forever.

We're All Standing in Line for That

Someone in Florida (always Florida) was caught selling
tickets to heaven for a hundred bucks. Drugs, Jesus,
outer space—the details don't matter, only the certainty
that nearly anyone would pay a hundred dollars
to get to heaven, and the surest way to get there
is to be dead. People don't like to talk about it,

but many of us think about being dead,
and how it just might be better than being alive.
In heaven surely the news doesn't slash you
with the screams of children pulled from parents
seeking asylum in one of the richest countries
in the world. In heaven surely we've all found
our purpose, and yes maybe that purpose is to take

the very best drugs anyone has ever imagined
and sit around chatting with Jesus, who must be
one hell of a guy if he said even a little
of that stuff about loving your neighbor and helping
the poor and heaven being a rich-asshole-free place
because no kind of camel is getting through the eye
of any kind of needle. Of course what do I know

about being dead? On my resume under Experience
it's all just living: watching my parents die
and my sister die and my brothers and me getting older
and none of us flying to outer space with the billionaires,
just trying to remember the old songs
so we have something to do while we're waiting.

Flock

I want to rush the world like my dog
rushes geese in the pond, as if I don't fear

what could happen. Instead I list my sins
against nature: I don't always buy

organic, I snatched fireflies and imprisoned
their magical bodies of light

in a jar when I was a child, I consume
flesh. Always the earnest Midwesterner,

my tongue fills with explanations
and excuses trying to spill over,

so afraid am I of judgments other
than my own. I curse starlings

sometimes, sleekly invasive, shiny
as salesmen. It's true I love

creatures that fly, but can anyone
love them all? June bugs flinging

themselves at you like hail, tangling
in your hair; sharp-winged smoke

warning of dead islands, doomed
air? When the geese rise up,

spread their wings, bugle their clamorous
warnings at my dog as she swims,

I wait until she hauls herself out,
shakes, noses my hand for a treat,

and then I say *good girl, good girl,*
expanding my praise to that citizen

army that didn't fly away but stayed
and, together, drove off the threat.

Noctalgia

The loss of dark skies is so painful, astronomers coined a new term for it
　　　　　　　　　　　　　　　　—headline 9/17/23

The country of my own past
seems oceans away, or just one step
under a mossy lintel into a fantasy
world I might have read in a book
held under my desk in eighth grade

before the teacher gently noted
even earnest kids like me needed
to pay attention in class. Kids like me
who weren't rich in money—
and how much that mattered
in the '80s, decade of Reaganomics

and bewildering designer brands—but
were college bound on brains and family
expectation. Page 172: a girl who likes
dogs and horses better than people

walks with friends across the campus
quad, the dark wind of October
blowing their eyes bright, hopeful.
Page 378 (I read long books):
students crowd a ping-pong table,
laptop keys clicking, asking questions

before they send their fledgling words
into the ether. Page 26: a raccoon kit
reaches into the rubber boot
of a ringleted child, barn door

open behind them. Please don't ask
about the 500s, when the protagonist's
sister dies and her last hope for wings
withers in hard frost. I honestly don't

want to make page 1000 with the world
as it is and my genetic inheritance
of fearful unrecognition, mind
gone awry inside a body that just

won't die. But perhaps the next
200 pages or so could contain
some green ease, less pain, more
floating. I try to remember I can
only read one page at a time
and shouldn't this be the one
where the once-girl is happy? I wish

for one of those weighted bookmarks
so lead-heavy they fall through
time so I can start the book again,
remembering to remember every
tender equine nose smelling of sweet
alfalfa, every sharp spark rising
into the distant, glittering sky.

Save What You Can

Diving across the concrete patio, I grab
one dog's collar while keeping hold
of the other. The fledgling—so small
I can't tell what species it is—chirps

and hops away into the grass. Fifty-
something isn't an age to be hurling
one's body down. Elbow, knee, ankle
bruise and swell like rising bread dough.

We had a horse when I was growing up
who loved my mother so much
that if she had a seizure and fell
he would stand over her and bare his teeth

at anyone approaching. This fierce chestnut
lowered his head so at six I could push his bridle
over his ears, opened his mouth for the bit.
So much tenderness in this world

even if the moon weeps nightly. I knew
I could save the baby bird
even though the first dog—a retriever—
had scooped it up in his mouth

because I could still hear it, muffled
but somehow echoing inside that toothy cage.
When my mother opened her eyes
to the sight of her horse's belly

she'd say *Move, you silly oaf,*
and he'd step over her as carefully
as you carry a brimming cup to the table,
never spilling a drop.

Grubby

Dust in our ears and nostrils conjured
by curry combs on winter-fuzzy equine coats.
Dog fur, calico cat multi-colored hair

and raccoon kit fluff soft as milkweed floss
clinging to our clothes. Weed seeds and cockleburs
embedded in sweatshirt sleeves and thick white socks

that I turned inside-out to keep the seams off
my sensitive toes. Mud encrusted sneakers
with once-white shoelaces—no sandals

allowed in the barn—and that holy smell
of musk and alfalfa, warmth and clover
on our hands and necks and faces

from leaning hard against our loves.
Sweat and leather oil where we sat
lazy on a broad back or proper in a saddle.

Manure when the stalls had to be mucked out,
though I was too small to use a pitchfork.
Grass stains on the knees of our jeans and sometimes

blood seeping through from a scrape. Leaves
decorating faded black velvet hardhats after a trail ride.
All the joy I knew back then was grubby.

Slog

Everything will work out for the best, fortune cookies
assure us, but I don't know what it feels like
to be optimistic. Do other people wake up
believing the three billion birds lost

from North America since 1970 will somehow
return? That our overheated air will cool to livable
before we find ourselves trapped on what were once
mountain peaks, islanded as Donne could never

have predicted? Do the undepressed keep
disaster at arm's length and live like bodhisattvas,
riding in a car catching and releasing the wind
with their hands out the window? I read once

that humans overestimate themselves and we need this
pretense, because who could go on if they believed
they were worse than average? I hammer myself
with advice for happiness: remember

the kind woman who works at the pet food store
and always says hello, tells you she'll pray for your sick
husband, and figure she'll never see his blasphemous
Flying Spaghetti Monster bumper sticker.

Speak to yourself as you would to a friend
or a child or a dog—*good girl, good beautiful girl.*
Take a breath all the way into the tiny alveoli
at the bottom of your lungs where the air can get

as stagnant as the green river you grew up beside,
and when you let it out, blow your worries down
that river's surface and out of sight
like gold fall leaves fading to winter.

Oh self. Knowing you can't control much
is like grabbing a knife in the dark. Maybe
everything will work out for the best because
we'll be gone and the world will have a chance

to start over, marrying cell to cell and getting it
right this time, building in hope like an air sac
future beings will use to buoy themselves in any
element. I guess until then I'm earthbound,

stuck in the slog with the rest of us, shoulder
to shoulder and taking turns leading the marching song.

Everybody Walks in England

At twenty-one I thought my body was
just a room I lived in, my mind the real
me where love ran clear as a beck

and birds flew over the horizon, dark
stars in a sunset sky. Then I got sick
and lost horses and softball and patience

with my own keening that sounds like
the high bell stuck mid-ring inside
my ears. I have stood on the moors

where Charlotte imagined Jane Eyre
fleeing the ruins of her paradise
and asked the wind to take me, this

once, away and through the bracken
and heather and even the stinging
nettles because my breath couldn't

carry me far or fast enough. Shame
a small seed uncurling when
the white-haired Yorkshire woman

stopped to share a kind word, her
face creased from smiling, and then
turned to climb towards a hilltop

with a view I wouldn't see. Lucky,
I will come back and back again
with a man born of these stone-strewn

paths. Unlucky, my fingers and toes
stiffen like old roots. One day
I may lay this body down in a sacred

stone circle and hope to wake, if I wake
at all, with my blood singing a new
wild song as strong as the cold North Sea.

Letter to My Mother, 17 Years Dead

Mom, I had breast reduction surgery and I keep wanting
to call you. You'd ask nurse-informed questions
and I'd know I was being looked after by a person much better
at that task than I have been myself. The marks of my own
caretaking live inside my skin: fat from my inability to resist
sugar, each bite of orange-infused chocolate
glowing like fairy food and magical enough to make me
forget, for a few seconds, the pain and fatigue
snaking through my body like medieval demons,
impossible to exorcise and grinning behind my eyes
at doctors who do not believe they exist. I would prefer
a different vice, a drug that carries me weaving and whooshing
through my days, but I can't drink alcohol anymore
and I don't know where to get the rest.

                                           I've been watching
a tv show set in the 1930s and I'm in love
with Corfu now, with these people who read and play
music, eat without their phones at the ready. Remember
putting on the record of *Peter and the Wolf* so we could imagine
the story, lying on blue-green carpet nearly as dark as the woods?
Remember spontaneous horseback rides, just
one of us asking *Do you want to?* That was your dream,
not Dad's, and every day I'm grateful for the too-short years
we had to live it. The show's about a widowed mother
with her four children and sometimes I pretend it's us,
the five of us muddling through without the dark lasso
of Dad's fear and anger.

                               You must have been so tired
when we left the farm. Afraid of ruin both financial
and physical. Convinced you were giving us something precious
with your sacrifice. How did he persuade you?
Gas prices rising. The energy crisis. Your health hollow

as a chocolate rabbit you refused to buy for our Easter baskets,
always choosing substance over appearance. Did he say
we'd be happier in town?

                             I know this plot. War is coming.
The tv family is English. No doubt they will go back
at the end, their life in Corfu fading as dreams do
under gray skies and falling bombs.

                             Surgery went fine.
I was, I'm told, hilariously repetitive in recovery:
Did you have fun watching videos for three hours? I asked
my husband, the one you never met, over and over. *I love you.*
You will not be surprised to learn that I'm so squeamish
I can barely look at the wounds, raw tracks that seem
ready to tear open and release the red bird
of my heart.

                        Why did I excise what your genes
and Dad's gave me? Maybe just once I wanted what was lost
to be a *good riddance*. Maybe I can make it a tradition,
off-loading something every year until I'm almost
two-dimensional enough to slip into the screen
with my Corfu family and set the needle on a spinning disk,
close my eyes as the notes drift through 90-year-old sunshine.

Depression as Invasive Species

science says you may have been planted
long before I was born   you grew
in my ancestors and fruited

spreading your seeds on the genetic dirt
of men and women who came
together to make the people
who came together to make

me   and some of those
people suffered great gouges
in the soil of themselves   churning up
their beautiful gardens like a renegade
plow   so those seeds took root and multiplied

their gray tendrils reaching out
through the generations to entangle
my mind   and oh I am so tired

of believing it is my fault
I jot down the same answers every week
on those forms that ask stupidly if you
experience little pleasure or interest
in normal activities instead of something
clearer like *do you feel*

how others seem to feel or *would you*
give your hands for a pill if it meant
you strolled through your life
instead of trudging

as if I pulled the rake across my own skin
and asked my blood to sustain
my parents' traumas and their
parents' and so on   come on

big D   let's go to the mountains
we'll hold hands   I'll breathe in
the smells of pine and clear streams
you'll do your kudzu trick and smother
it all

Talking

Once I complimented a poet and he said, "It's all lies."

When one friend tries to sleep, her mind is like my neighbor's border collie, circling the yard, looking for imaginary sheep.

I used to carry rocks in my pocket because my often-angry father liked them, because he said, "See that stripe of red there? Isn't it beautiful?"

When I moved from a small town, my friend said, "Oh, I'm so glad you're moving to a city!" As if that were a good thing.

I am so very tired of men taking up so much space on the sidewalk.

How the bully starlings swoop down onto the bird feeder and all the other birds scatter.

How different we all are, as different as below and above water.

I do not understand you. I do understand you, but I am not like you. I like you, but I don't want to be like you.

Every day the earth rotates so only part of it is lonely at any given time.

This World Always Offers Reasons for Despair

war   again   in places where
people already have   too many stones
children suffering like   the dog
I saw a man   hitting   with a metal rod
at the off-leash park   that's usually
my haven

how can we   take care   of them?

in my own head   a wrongness   a well
endless and raw   nothing dropped
will ever hit bottom   I am not
even sad   just lost to myself   or
rather   part of me curls   on the blue
linoleum   of my childhood kitchen
pain   boiling over on the stove

this morning   late October
the light   creeping down
sideways   as if reluctant
to touch our   earth
my legs carrying me   undirected
(automatic   like some guns)   because
my dogs must   be walked
lest they break   the peace   of the house

I spot   a blue jay
sky-colored   strident   far from innocent
why was that ravenous bird   made
so beautiful   I do not want   to love it

My Anger Is a Thunderhead

one of those clouds building
like an anvil about to drop on the world
smashing sidewalks and bodies and the sweet
dry sense that everything's okay   fuck

chronic illness and the prisoner inside with her tiny spoon
tunneling through my nerves and sinews, my precious muscles
and the patience I was born with   fuck the virus and genetics

and cosmic japes that mean my toes throb and burn and even
wiggle without permission like I'm trying
to play an invisible piano with my feet   proper fuck
the ghost gulping my energy

so I have to lie. fucking. down. after I walk
the dogs or vacuum one single room or make gingerbread
cookies for my husband who can't eat the store-bought ones
because a pandemic virus knobbed him too

fuck capitalism and its sick arrogance
testosterone coating everything
in the sour taste of competition   fuck human reproductive
prowess and the slithering entitlement that makes us all

assume we deserve to live this way
that's killing everything   fuck the culture
decreeing the most money and respect
go to the lucky or the assholes

using other people's souls as their personal stepping-stones
across to the Shore of Repulsive Wealth
held up by the poor dogpaddling with their hands over their heads

never seeing sunlight   fuck knee-jerk conservatism
and its gagging cologne of mulish outrage
against reusable bags and free school lunches and adults

loving any other consenting adult they want to love
and doing whatever they want to do with their own bodies
and *inclusion* for goddess' sake   fuck anti-intellectualism

and anti-reading and anti-nuance   fuck the dickheads
who think women are dolls and the poison that makes women believe
they never deserved to be their whole glorious selves anyway

fuck the cancer that took my sister in her 50s
and the doctors whose fatphobia meant they didn't look
for the tumors behind her nausea and labored breath
so we could have had more
than nine months from diagnosis   fuck judgment, criticism,

comparison   fuck the fear that I'll overcome my melancholy
just in time to die, before I get to live
in a part of the world I don't hate   fuck looming civil war

and those fomenting it   fuck the thick chemical smell
of my neighbor's fabric softener gassing my yard
so I have to flee inside to breathe   fuck telling people they're not

permitted to have feelings because *first world problems* and fuck
being nasty to servers and clerks and fuck my guilt over this
rant because who said I wasn't allowed to get mad?

The Metaphorical Dog

Chasing the shadows of leaves, rolling in real
mud, the metaphorical dog doesn't have a name

and doesn't need one. She knows more about the sky
than any human alive: how it spins, a tall vase

shaped and reshaped by vast hands, blue to light
blue to midnight blue to pink orange gray red

and all the blues slippery as waves. *There's always
a dog in your poems,* a friend once told me, *though*

sometimes it's metaphorical. The metaphorical dog
lives more in her body every moment

than I do over the whole long cycle of a day,
plopping her rump suddenly to the ground

so she can scratch her silky ear, every motion
joyous and fluent. She carries Whitman's best lines

in her mouth, drops them at my feet and looks up,
panting her doggy laugh. Am I a poem, despite

my cloak of failures? She won't say, her tail
shedding stars as she trots away, each wag

throwing off drops of light from her swim
in the river most of us are still seeking a map for

down unlikely alleyways, under velvet concert seats,
outside our doors when we open them in the morning.

This Is the Tying of Shoes

The two bunny ears, one bending
down and through, and then around again,

before pulling both ears tight. The second
loop a trick our mother taught

to keep shoes from coming untied
and as far as I know none of us

ever tripped on an undone shoelace.
I thought we were remarkably unbroken—

no casts for any of us. But then
I remember: my oldest brother losing

a chunk of his calf when he tried
to break up a dog fight; my fall

from a tree, stitches, concussion;
my other brother's eyebrow cut

during a game involving hurled
dirt clods and the curtain

of blood he described; my sister's
fall from a horse, the six days of her

unconsciousness, me too young to know
how worried I should be. Our mother

also taught us the physical art
of joy in movement: throwing and running,

scooping grain from the feedbox, oiling
and polishing leather saddles and bridles.

That to live a life you cannot stop,
that you must use every trick you have

to remember play, that a body is not a tool
but a song that needs to be constantly sung.

There Are Things About Horses

I've always known,
since I first sat on a warm, wide back at two:
talk to and touch a horse

as you walk around behind him; stick your thumb
in the space between teeth towards the back of his mouth
to make him open up for the bit;

tighten the girth just before you get on
because a horse will hold his breath
to swell his middle when you're saddling him;

always mount from the left.
My pubescent years didn't require any knowledge
of horse-lore, just the mating

calls of thirteen-year-old boys who spoke loudly
of *fingering* and being *horny* on the bus
home from school, taunting me and my stack

of books held tight to my chest.
So much low-grade misery
the years just after we left the farm are marked

in memory by only a few grainy images.
Why is it no one ever tells you
all the ways you learned to tame your life

will fail again and again, no matter what you do
there will be times you're riding bareback
and bridleless across a treacherous landscape?

Quitter

I quit high school softball and volleyball,
the other girls sleek as otters
and me unversed in the arts of makeup

and hairspray. I quit track before that, my body
growing thicker and top-heavy, sheer mulish
stubbornness failing to propel me any faster,

my dream of flying over the high jump
thudding to earth. I quit law school, trading
torts for poems after I wrote limp lines

about the streaked hair of the boy who sat in front
of me; all I remember from that semester
is the word *thaumaturgical*. I quit love

after love because I was so damned
afraid, though I told myself otherwise. I quit
singing. I quit hoping. I quit reading

Chinese horoscopes because they always said
a person born in the year of the monkey was
easily discouraged. Some things I tried to quit

and couldn't: chocolate, poetry, living. The trees
aren't quitting when they let go
of their gilded leaves. Still, *quitter* is carved

in my flesh, grown over so only I
know it's there. Maybe this is why, of all
the stories, the ones I love keep going back

to a younger world, each magical path stretching
ahead of the girl carrying stars in her throat,
nothing yet decided, nothing yet left behind.

Flyover Country

Central Illinois wears a rich brown coat
beaded with emerald corn and soybeans, gold

winter wheat and fine rolled bales of hay. Narrow
roads run straight so even if you're lost you know

you're traveling in one of the cardinal
directions. My parents let me skip

detasseling, having watched my three siblings
get up before dark in the still damp heat

of July to ride a flatbed pulled by a tractor
and pull off feathery tassels so no wild

pollination could ruin the seed corn. How many
Midwestern kids earned their tuition in those

sweaty weeks working dawn to dusk and falling
into bed only to get up and do it again?

I smelled the exhaustion rising off my siblings
and chose my first job: shelving books

in the graduate library where it was cool
and dark and teeming with words. Sometimes

the gold letters stamped into a cloth cover
spoke of poetry; I befriended Sara Teasdale

under fluorescent lights, cross-legged on concrete.
Oh beauty, are you not enough? Why am I crying

after love? Sixteen and stirred by spells of romance,
I had no idea where the storms and doldrums

of my search for the perfect kiss would take me.
I still remember the first time I lifted off

in a plane over those patchwork fields—my first
love, my truest, the one I would never tire of.

Time Is Not Real, but Scientists Say It Makes No Difference to Us

My mother is still alive. My mother is having a seizure and I am six. She falls to the ground and adults push-pull me away so I cannot see. My mother is dying of pancreatic cancer. My mother is steering the canoe from the stern, her paddle nearly silent as we glide past swans, giant as ghosts. My mother is riding horses. My mother is reading books about how to ride and care for horses. My mother is teaching me how to sew, my sister how to cook. My mother is holding a newborn puppy like a glass vase. My mother is watching the Olympics on television, her wonder infecting us all. My mother is flying in some other world, maybe riding a flying horse, maybe her beloved big red horse, the one who stands guard over her when she has a seizure and snaps at anyone who approaches, the one who lowers his head and opens his mouth for the bit so I can slip his bridle over his ears. Every day all at once she is doing these things. Every day of my childhood she is falling and riding and loving animals and singing outside. Her curly hair is falling into her eyes and she is pushing it back so she can see.

Passage

Don't we take birds for granted, their easy leaving,
how ghosts adhere to their every appearance?
My grandfather coaxing chickadees

to eat from his hand. My mother paging through
dog-eared identification books, full of illustrations
and the words to avian tunes. My sister

pointing out hawks perched along the highway.
Truly we're surrounded by the dead, walking
or driving or sitting around in our back yards

so absorbed in our phones we don't even notice
the wing whistles of mourning doves
warning of some danger seen or sensed.

And now we're starting September, speeding
towards the season of dark. Already the geese begin
their high calling, gathering their spirits

for the journey south. Do you remember
the first time you heard them, standing outside
in a pink dusk, realizing the world was stranger

than you had known and more seductive, to pull
even the adults from dinner to tilt their heads back
and watch the dark runes moving on without you?

Parfumerie Magique

I've only shopped for scents a few times
in my life, out of place in my unlabeled jeans and t-shirts,

but this establishment is irresistible. The bell rings
as I step inside and there it is in a chestnut-colored

bottle: *Eau de Velvet Horse Nose*, the smell
of uncomplicated love. And here's *Aroma of a Dog's Cheek*:

interdependence, solace. My friend picks up a bold red vial
labeled *Being Right and Everyone Acknowledging It*,

and if she doesn't buy it for herself, I will.
For everyday, I suspect she'll select *Cold Brew with Cream*.

I once worked in a library shelving books,
the most optimistic years of my life, so *Dusty Tomes*

nearly leaps into my hand. The shelves moved
in that library, gliding on electric runners, startling

when I was working at night and a coworker
pranked me. Maybe they even have

My Worst Fear is a Library Ghost, because these days
Yeats' rough beast crowds the edges of my vision

no matter where I look. Maybe I should just
infiltrate the factory and churn out only *Peace Perfume*,

send it up in planes to be dropped like fabulous bombs
over the whole suffering earth. And what might that

smell like? Spring sunlight, chocolate fondue,
mint leaves, twin fawns hopping on their too-long legs,

with base notes of fresh beginnings and flight, the smooth
blues of the air caressing you every day you're alive.

My Mother at the Sweet Corn Festival

was more beautiful than a shiny new John Deere
harvester, all teeth and joy, rows of sweet pale kernels

succumbing to her onslaught of love. You wouldn't have known
she grew up in a classy suburb of D.C., went to the Cathedral's

private girls' school, still knew her way up to the choir loft
twenty-five years later. The priest scolded her but not too hard

when he caught us, me a little girl and her grinning
like the mischievous child she never stopped being.

When she lifted a saddle onto a horse's back, stuck
her thumb in the safe spot between his front and back teeth

to make him open his mouth for the bit,
I tried to imagine her wearing white gloves

to church, sitting demurely with her ankles crossed.
I couldn't. She belonged in corn and soybean country

like I did, where the tv showed hard-working farmers
enjoying yields provided by chemical fertilizers

with names that slipped off their not-quite-Southern
country tongues like melted butter. She said

care-a-mell instead of *car-ml*, made sure we
said *roof* with the *coo* of a mourning dove. If only

our father had gone off on a business trip and never
come home, we might all have been happy,

our giggles painting the walls of that house
the color of an expelled breath that had been held

too long. Or maybe not. Who understands the complex equations
of family, geography, decade? My father used to say

Did you know she ate twelve ears of corn
at the festival one year? I wish I could go back

now to analyze their expressions and body language
to see if he was fondly teasing or pressing the thorn

into her tender skin every time, if she thought
it was as funny and wonderful as we did, proud

children hoping to match her record one day, or if
her face revealed the concern that he had really wanted

a wife who cooked and cleaned like his own mother,
behaved like a quiet ornament. If she could

have found him one, I believe she would have
presented her like a gift to us all. It is hard

to find corn that good outside the Midwest, but
every time I hold a fresh steamed ear to my mouth

I close my eyes and pray to the gods of vast square fields
under fiery July skies that this time will be the one.

I'd Still Go Back

I see that time in images flashing like sun on water:
the raspberry patch and my mother pointing out
a leaf, calling it "katydid," my nickname, then suddenly
it grew legs and menaced like a grasshopper.

My sister, mother, and me on a trail ride, dusty summer,
the mountain of matted fur called King greeting us
as we passed his yard, following the horses for a while. I
loved that dog, sewed him inside my body, took him

to every lonely place I slept for years
and years. Wind roughing the barn
while my brother and I climbed too high
and half-fell, half-jumped to the dirt floor, freezing

at the sight of a rusty spike from the manure-spreader
inches from my neck—just one way we brushed sleeves
with death, looking back after passing by to see
if we should apologize. I was troubled—weren't we

all?—and one night, sleepwalking, rose from my twin bed,
padded down the stairs and out into the snowy back yard
to feed the horses. My sister caught me before I reached
the barn, steered me back to our warm room. All I remembered

in the morning was the certainty I'd left
something vital undone. You can trap water
in your cupped hands but the light slips off
to gild another wavelet. My first ten years looked like

an ordinary childhood, where grubby kids ran home
to a green-painted house and washed the blood off
skinned knees before a dinner of spaghetti and sauce
made of our own garden's tomatoes. It was

a knife-throwing contest, a low rushing flight across prairies,
an ecosphere in a glass jar, the frenzied crescendo
at the end of a symphony or fireworks display—almost
too loud, too bright, too much, and then—nothing.

Yesterday I Read About the Climate Crisis,

despair leaching into my bones, poisoning everything. All
the sci-fi I read as a kid coming true, and I don't want to live
in those worlds.

Today I wake to my joints blaring
like tuneless trumpets, muscles proclaiming weakness and a love
of the easy chair. Here's to black tea with milk and willpower,

moving my traitor body despite it all. Loading up the dogs,
holding my curses at fumbled buckles under my tongue.
On the car radio, a podcast about the ancient Romans,

their Etruscan rulers. Anything but the past hundred years,
the next hundred, all the harrowing news of our self-made
doom. I brake hard for a robin in the road, pull into my usual spot.

And then—miracle!—the park is glorious with wind,
hot Memphis summer morning awash with the kind of air that lifts
the me inside and I am light, light as my mother's grin when she

urged her big chestnut horse over the jumps he loved. I remember
flying, back in the 70s when we could have done something. But
dogs romp and dash, swallows skim the grasses, green

swells my lungs. Oh, Earth, we both may be ruins of ourselves,
but let us stay a little while yet, sipping what secret joy
the universe still sees fit to offer.

What the Insomniac Thinks

When my shoulders touch the sheets, the sleep
that had rubbed its warm fur against my ankles

while I sat on the couch after dinner
dissolves. So my mind takes up this challenge

and posits humans eating hot wings because we want
to fly, and suddenly there's a woman chasing

moths and stuffing them in her mouth, her body
hollowing, attracting fairy dust. And do we

eat fish to belong in the cradle of water,
potatoes to know the darkness

with its roads of mycorrhizae connecting
everything? And how many of us have wondered

if fungus underlies existence, mushroom trips
showing exactly what's real? Some time later

beings of light—clear vessels filled with magnitude—
bend over me as I garden, hold my hands

holding the trowel, as if to make sure what grows
is right and good and even magic. How else

to describe the profound strangeness that is sleep
but as a sort of magic, a compost

in which we deposit the scraps of the waking world
and hope for the nourishment we need to go on?

My Father the Unlikely Buddhist

My father left me a wooden statue of Kuan Yin, bodhisattva
of compassion, with her hand on the back of a lion. The gold
paint is partly gone, the age-darkened wood showing through
like shadows. He was a servant of beauty, would have thrived
tending the statues in some quiet temple, sitting in meditation

and imagining a glittering afterlife with curved lines
like a river stone. Instead he polished his worries smooth
with repetition, certain he'd be penniless, his children
would fall from whatever tree we happened to climb,
cars would smash and—what? I'm not sure he feared death.

It was pain and ruin he dreaded, a breaking of the established
order. Change itself, stampeding towards him. I try
to understand him so I may understand myself. How my hands
strangle the steering wheel. How my nightmares leave me jobless
and begging, unable to remember in what state I live now.

Sometimes I think the great sorrow of my father's life
was having children, the whole messy houseful of us,
only four but multiplied by noise and dirt into tortuous
chaos. But then I remember him laughing, surprise
rising from his belly, a deep bubble of sound that made us all

laugh too until our faces were red and he was wiping
the tears from his eyes—my father, more bear than stag.
I hope that when he left his body he was given a choice.
Kuan Yin rests her hand on the back of the lion, but he
looks at her like there is nothing more beautiful in all the worlds.

Bartleby, What Would You Make of the 21st Century?

A friend sends me a message via social media
to say that she's in hospice
and I'm as stunned as if her words had come by dragon,

sinuous body flaming across the sky over my subdivision
of brick-faced houses and brown winter lawns.
Is this where we live now, the screen

flashing words from someone so close
to death I want to ask her to look out
for my sister? I tell her I am so glad

to know her, careful not to slip
into past tense. She writes again to say
she is trying to finish her memoir. She doesn't

say *while she can*, but I hear it. I don't know
her well but I know she's no coward. The only time
we met in person we hugged, her older body thin

in my fleshy arms. I have so many words
they pile up by my feet like snow,
but my sister was in hospice for less

than a week. This memoir will never
be finished. The cursor blinks and blinks, hungry,
until I sigh and close the laptop. In my mud-soaked

back yard the birds land at the feeder,
their delicate ancient claws like the scritch
of pen on paper, their wings like the rustle of pages.

Line Up

I loved school, the words and the numbers,
my fourth-grade teacher, Mr. B.,
who let me work through the math book
at my own pace, checked my paper, shook
his head, and twirled my pigtail once
like a more playful father than my own.

I even forgave him for lining up us kids sometimes
by calling those with the lowest scores first,
then the second lowest, and so on

until it got to me and he said, "Eggheads
can go now." Looking back, I wonder
at the strategy: how did those kids
feel, standing in the light of failure
but finally not being punished for it?

I wish I had learned what Mr. B.
perhaps unintentionally
implied, this man with his auburn '70s mustache—

that test scores weren't a guarantee
the world would move me to the front,
that failing wasn't shame

but inescapable, like pushing open
the door to the fifth-grade classroom in August,

where the stern unsmiling teacher
sat behind her desk, her rules

as unforgiving as the lines we were supposed
to write our names within, or else.

What I Wish for in the Dark

Mom drove us away from the lights of town
and out into the creaking cornfields, though not as far
as the rural area where we'd grown up, playing

flashlight tag with neighborhood kids
through the humid summer nights.
Olly-olly-in-come-free, the loser yelled,

announcing he was found by *it*
so the rest of us, the best at hiding, emerged
like young magicians from the shadows.

But we had been living in town for a year,
limited to patches of sod and pavement
watched by strangers who thought kids

should not be out after dark. Mom missed
the farm too, must have felt her life tightening
like a scarf tied and tied again around her throat.

And so when the Perseids came that August
we lay on a blanket beside the tall green corn
looking for the Milky Way, looking for the flash

of a shooting star to wish on. When the man
stopped his car to ask if we were okay—
two preteen kids and a woman on the side

of a blacktop road in the dark—I swallowed
my wish and it went down hard as a fresh
peppermint disc. I'm not saying I haven't had

a lucky life: sun-warmed raspberries like fistfuls
of rubies, dogs offering their silken trust,
the knowledge that at least one person loved me

every day of my life. We didn't see any
burning meteorites that night, or if we did
I don't remember. I think Mom was trying

to remind herself and us that the same stars rode
the heavens no matter where we lived,
that we had not lost the sky. Even now

I look up, choose a small light
sent like a beacon from too far away to touch
and speak what I want for myself, what I want

for a world stuck like us in the stern current of time.

The Barred Owls

call in their monkey way,
fog prowls the neighborhood,

and on my phone I see my niece
texted at 5:30 to say

they had to put their curly mutt, fourteen,
to sleep—small, oddly put together dog

with front feet that turned out
like a dancer in plié—and she hoped

her other aunt, my sister, would take care of him
in heaven. No morning will ever start

like this again, and who should I thank
or curse for that? Once upon a time

my niece pretended to be a dog
to get my attention. I was not

the aunt who scooped her up
for tickles, explained the rules

of games so she, the youngest, could play
with her older siblings. Now she is

a mother, now she has broken herself
and made a kaleidoscope, her pieces forming

and re-forming a new beauty
time and again. I don't know

what the owls are saying, but I hope
they are calling all our lost souls home.

To Myself at Twelve

Here is what you need to know: you will never
get the farm back, though you will dream of it
for decades. In each dream, the farm
will be different: half underwater, or a town
grown up around it, or the barn and arena full

of the detritus of a fairground. In some dreams
the horses are different but still waiting for you.
Always the undone with you, the responsibility
that sent you out in the snow, sleepwalking,
to feed the horses at three a.m. And your sister

following, stopping you, bringing you back
inside the house. She's the one who, years after
you've forgotten how to ride a horse, will have
her own farm. Hard to believe but you won't love it,
the place too saturated with her husband's anger—

so like your father's you will be transported
back to this age and the fear and rage that roots you
to the spot, frozen as winter topsoil. Oh, don't
worry. You will find easier love and feel it ebb
and flow, perplexed by its oceanic nature,

how it scrapes and reshapes everything.
I am so sorry you won't know whether to throw
yourself in or retreat to the shore, and so
you will sometimes do one when you should
have done the other. Eventually there will be

marriage—twice—but you will be relieved
to know: no children. You were right
that it is hard enough to raise yourself.
The world with its love affair with money
and prestige will carve away at the spindle

of you until some places are so thin
they barely hold. And when you think
there is little left to mark you
your sister will get cancer and die
between one spring and the next. My

darling. You will hurt like a tree struck
by lightning. The pain and the burning
will find you again and again. Every time,
every single damned time, you will step out
of the blackened trunk, back into this world.

I don't know how you will do it, I still don't know,
but there is something in you as bright and hard
as a diamond. Without that we would not both
still be here, standing on either side of the river,
watching each other breathe in the morning light.

My Mother's Other Life

I would give her a childhood with horses
and hills to ride them in,
the clear wind racing her centaur-self.

No brother, just sisters who show her
how to skip a rock, tie a rope and swing
out over the water, to move in the world

like someone who will be a doctor one day.
A father who lives, who tells her
she gets this life just once and to hell

with those who don't like the way she lives it.
A mother whose anger burns out quickly,
who reads to her and laughs and laughs. No white

gloves. No world shouting good girls
don't love other girls. A wife
who loves her for breaking

into song, for the ski slope
of her nose, for how she starts
water fights with their children

and fifteen projects she will never finish.
A hardhat for every ride
so those children never have to know

what to do when their mother has a seizure.
A house made of logs in Colorado
or northern California, enough space

for the stray teenagers who find
their way there, for the children who,
like us, always come back. Pralines

whenever she wants them, and if
she must die, an appetite for sweetness
right up to the end, when her first horse

comes trotting through the bedroom door
and she climbs onto his broad back,
crossing to the next country with a grin.

Shell

Inside my flesh, the bones of my hand spread out
like a cactus. Beyond that, the pebbles and sticks

of the wrist. Medicine cannot tell me
why I ache, and I do not hurt enough

to pay for specialists and their complex tests.
Still the pain has become a companion

of my days, reminding me to touch things
differently, with care and attention,

like a Buddhist at daily tasks: each one
as important as the other, grounded

in the present moment, not the semi-conscious
routine through which we dream of the future

or the past. How rarely do I live
from the inside out, loving my bones

and muscles, my blood vessels with their efficient
traffic, the microscopic cities of cells

and the transient hormones and nutrients.
I should call my body *wonder*, worship

it with offerings and wrap it in silk.
Instead it is my vehicle, my shell, reminder

of a past that felt more holy,
a future with a final ending. Come now,

hands. Do your job. Stroke the fur,
pull on the boots, grasp the bird feeder

with its many portals. Idle only
when I am sleeping. In return I will offer you

to my love and he will raise you to his lips,
kiss your palm, remind you that all this is just enough.

The Afterlife of Dogs

is where the party's at, the tail-swinging
nose-first howl of a time we all dream of

deep in the old houses of our animal bodies
where the earth is so close we can taste

puppyhood again. The dance floor's
all play bows and prancing and neck

bites and there ain't no food table
just big bowls of chicken and sausages

refilling themselves forever.
The afterlife of dogs stretches huge

across every idea of heaven
and the doors stand open to any

size or shape, breed or color. Maybe you
can fly in your afterlife and that's ok

but you're going to want to lie down
in the dogs' meadow where the sun

warms fur and the smells are winged
jewels everyone can see. I'll tell you

the truth, I can't remember when I
didn't fear suffering, when the future

didn't seem like a steamroller-sized mail truck
loaded with danger on glossy cardstock.

I try to remember my body's the fucking galaxy
and so is yours. And long after this

trudge through the sleet in too-thin shoes
may something of us still be around

to watch all the good boys and good girls
roll and shake on the bank of the river of stars.

How Lucky

I want to wake up every morning to news as toothsome
as those macarons we bought in the Eiffel Tower

on our two-years-after-the-wedding honeymoon,
so light and chewy we never had any better

despite our doubts about getting them where every tourist goes.
Once daily I want to read a poem that leaves

an imprint on my mind like the feet of the coffee table
leave circles in the rug to show where it should be

replaced after vacuuming. I want to look for my husband
and find him cleaning out the garage like he's been

meaning to do for years, miraculously recovered from his long
post-viral illness, making jokes about the six pairs

of worn, mud-covered sneakers and the spiders they shelter.
I want to open my back door to acres of wild land

crossed with paths for easy walking, and for my dogs
to leap into the streams and come out sparkling

and for not one chemical to be sprayed or leaked there
from now until forever, all the plants and animals,

furred or feathered or too small to see with the naked eye
singing amen like a vast choir. And when the burning gets close,

when we're not even hiding in breath-held basements
anymore but just looking around to feed our eyes

all the wonder we still can, I want to sit eating ice cream
with people I love, everyone accepting another scoop, another,

chocolate and caramel and strawberry and peanut butter
and mint chocolate chip running down our faces

like tears, laughing because there's no more
worry, tomorrow isn't coming and what we've lost

can't be recovered even if we had all the magic
we dreamed, as children, we might have

some day. It seems to me no matter what it's mixed with
loss always tastes sweet, tastes like what we once had—all that love!—

so good the goosebumps rise on our arms. How lucky we were
to have had it, this mother/father/sister/brother/earth, this everything.

About the Author

Katherine Riegel's most recent book is a lyric memoir about her sister and grief, *Our Bodies Are Mostly Water* (Cornerstone Press, 2025). Her previous collections of poetry are *Love Songs from the End of the World* (Main Street Rag, 2019), *Letters to Colin Firth* (Winner of the Sundress Publications Chapbook Competition, 2015), *What the Mouth Was Made For* (FutureCycle, 2013), and *Castaway* (FutureCycle, 2010). Her poems have appeared in *Poets Reading the News*, *Rattle*, *SWWIM*, *Thimble*, and elsewhere. Co-founder and managing editor of *Sweet* (sweetlit.org), she runs online writing classes in poetry and flash creative nonfiction.

Find her at katherineriegel.com and in southern Scotland, where she moved in summer 2025 with her British husband, two Golden Retrievers, and two cats.

S
Sheila-Na-Gig Editions